WHAT IS A WOMAN

WHAT IS A WOMAN

CASSIDY SILVERWOOD

QuillQuest Publishers

CONTENTS

1 Definition of Woman   1

2 Gender Identity   5

3 Feminism   9

4 Stereotypes and Misconceptions   14

5 Women's Rights   18

CHAPTER 1

Definition of Woman

According to many around the world, a woman is an adult female human being. To say that woman means adult female human being is to say that the word "woman" can be analyzed or defined in terms of the words "adult," "female," and "human being." This may seem trivial, because the word woman consists of the words "wo-" and "man," that is, the word "man" is contained in the word "woman," and adult female human beings are composed of the femaleness that is contained in the word "woman." The idea tends to be opposed on the basis of a division between social constructionists or anti-essentialists, as they are commonly called, who deny essences, and natural kind theorists, who allow that essences exist, whether or not individuals have met them. Some might suggest that the problem of defining concept is more philosophical than the problem of defining words, but this is not the case.

The question of what a woman is has been considered from a variety of perspectives. As with the question of what a man is, an answer to the question depends on what one means by "woman." However, the answer given in a particular context is often assumed to be the only one or the most important one. Furthermore, an answer given in one context is often misunderstood as an answer to which must be the more important question of what most women fundamentally are. The first section of this essay examines the ways in which the question of what a woman is has been answered.

1.1. Biological characteristics

The current landscape of reproductive technologies gives evidence of the importance of the difference between men and women in terms of the ability to procreate and, generally, a different value is put by families in the anteriority of the gestation, maintaining the essential and indissoluble link between the biological mother and her baby. The division can help some family constellations in their desire to have children through gestational surrogates, hence, although not all infertile people use reproductive technologies, it is crucial to consider whether a woman can decide whether she wants to gestate the embryo herself, or choose the gestation of another.

Women can get pregnant. This is a trait that is biologically tied to women. To be more specific, women are the only humans that can get pregnant and give birth to a baby without being a donor for the mother or the embryo. There is no clear explanation for why evolution has allowed for this phenomenon to exist in human females alone. In many species there is no difference in this respect, being any female unique in this capacity. Some authors explain this difference by appealing to Homo sapiens ability for childcare, and suggest that this is the result of a co-evolution between female and infants in modern humans, assuming that women offer unique opportunities to the survival of their infants, and that helpless babies create unique links with women.

1.2. Social roles

The many possibilities in the abilities of a single person are limited by the linking of several social roles. A person can only perform those tasks, the union of social roles which is approximately relevant. The distribution of life roles in accordance with age and sex plays an important role in upholding traditional gender roles. However, in Latvia, the distribution of age-related roles is not strictly in line with the traditional concept of women and men – there are significantly fewer women than there are men who are actively involved in work.

A social role influences whether a woman will have time to participate in political debates, go to the sauna, have time to conduct research an hour a day, go somewhere once in a while, or simply have time to relax. Social roles, where men are seen as providers, and women are seen primarily as mothers, especially reinforce such expectations. If a woman who has not taken on the role of "wife" is accepted within society almost without question, then in the case of a woman who has not taken on the role of "mother", society has a poll after which the hostility shows if the fourth or even fiftieth time the woman refuse to carry out the role of a woman (the role of a wife does not impose such strict deadlines).

1.3. Historical perspectives

Furthermore, in his essay Politics, attributed to Aristotle, is foreseen the predominance of men as being originated from the fact that: "it becomes manifest that everywhere man governs woman". This truth is also shown by the animals of male and of female sex: even the ones have the control over the others, the mature must have their horseshoes; this is a certain sign of the nature and of which the lord and the one who is subject of the governing. This principle is getting even clearer: also among the animals who live set free man has the command over woman; and this one cannot do anything without an eye on that one...she is even more willing to serve woman rather than to man...It can be also topically logically deduced that the set free man is by nature more ruler than woman, the boy than the girl, by the adult than the child, and the elder rather than the younger; supremacy is based also on them. And had it not been due to the harm, they would not have disagreed on this order of importance.

Historical perspectives - Aristotle's Second Sex: Unlike in the ancient Hellenic, Spartan, Pythagorean and Athenian Republic laws women were (sexually) freer and, at least in these 3 cities, faiths were matriarchal, in his Laws Plato legalized heterosexual love but without consequently erotic act between the same sexes. In his second Book, Aristotle tells that: "not even with what we call the irrational beings does she (woman) possess the virtue that is to govern, namely, the virtue that is unique to body, a virtue as such. For when she gets involved in its passions and propels them or against them, she has no virtue, she acts disproportionately and against justice. So, she is governing, but not as a slave". As to woman "to her what is proper is to be submissive".

CHAPTER 2

Gender Identity

Nevertheless, the sex/gender distinction has been critiqued by some feminists who worry that if sex is natural, it will be assumed that femininity is just natural, something forced on women through their biological nature, which means that a focus on change in gender will dissipate. Even though Simone de Beauvoir seemed to argue that femininity is natural, arguing for becoming a woman, rather than being born one. Further, the distinction has been critiqued by some for claiming that sex is objective and material, while gender cultural and psychological, leaving no room for transgender individuals who know profoundly inside that they want to live as another gender, unlike those who are simply performing gender. However, most feminists find the critiques mistaken. A feminist focus on gender is explained by the fact that mistakes about sex are never discovered from the world, since sexed bodies are themselves cultural concepts. Sex differences, as the socially constructed ideas that organize perception and biological data, are not, in themselves, proof that gender and sex do not belong in the same spectrum. The sex/gender distinction is simply a way to show that one's bodily existence is not private and instead, a social project of the construction of a gender.

The sex/gender distinction is fundamental for understanding debates about what it means to be a woman and about changing the legal definition of women. It refers to the distinction traditionally drawn by feminists and others between what is biological, namely, one's sex, and what is socially constructed, namely, one's gender. This distinction was famously used by Simone de Beauvoir in her book The Second Sex, where she argued that a baby girl was initially constructed as different from others and then confirmed as feminine and lesser.

2.1. Cultural influences

Machismo with the social and moral conception that women, by nature, are different from men in many ways. This differentiation should be a starting point for "segregating" them, prevented them from expressing their true potential as well as to live together with men, in all spheres, with equity and mutual respect. In addition to the vast social implications, machismo encompasses different dimensions of the individuals, who internalize their values from childhood, and it is not uncommon for the individual, men, or women, to say that machismo does not exist since it is saturated with the psyche. This perspective gained strength in psychodynamics, considering prejudice as a personality characteristic and ignoring the context from which it emerged. In this perspective, the mother would educate children.

The expectations are so widespread today that they never stand out as the cultural imposition they are. Being a mother, cooking, and doing the housecleaning have been the main attributes of women in all times. Even today, with the increasingly widespread female participation in the job market. The society stigmatizes who is employed by neglecting their "duties" of maintaining the marriage and the children. It is not that a man should not take on his responsibilities, but one thing can never be forgotten, they are responsibilities of woman. After all, what kind of society considered a beautiful and well-kept woman, who in addition to performing all her duties, maintains excellent professional performance? So the woman's role associated with dated attributes, is much more recent than we believe, since it depends on cultural influences and values of society.

2.2. Personal experiences

Where did this knowledge of being a girl come from? I don't know. I sometimes question what my motives are in the decisions I made. If a biological woman made exactly the same choices in life as I did: becoming an engineer, writing about her experiences to raise consciousness, marrying a biological man, playing no professional sports, and so forth, no one would have any question but that she was a woman. Being a transsexual woman, for me, is my most personal experience. It is exceedingly difficult to convey in words. There are days when I feel that blood drains from my hands and I see myself and others in the world as desiring little more than flesh and violence. Other times there is no boundary between the shifting snow and the burning mountain, and I know that everybody and everything around me is simply my dream. I love them, and I am their nightmare. The angry looks, the fear and guilt on people's faces as they shift to outer makes me feel like I must be incredibly monstrous and cruel. I only sometimes feel like a woman, I never do not think and feel like a transsexual woman. I often wonder if I'd have all of these experiences if I were a biological woman? I know I would not have the same ones.

I always knew, as long as I can remember, that I was a girl or a person who was supposed to be a girl. I can recall this knowledge going back to when I was about three, and my life has always been based on this knowledge. I played house with the other girls.

I discussed "Who would be the mother?" with my young friends when we went someplace in a group and the only people present were other children. I fell in love with young men, dated, and was married. But I always knew that I was a girl. I remember playing house with the other girls when I was about four, and the look of incredulous wonder in the eyes of my parents when they discovered what we were doing. For a while after that, playing house or dolls became something we could be punished for doing. When I was quite sure I was alone in the house I used to put a towel on my head and sweep with a rumpled up apron tied to my waist.

CHAPTER 3

Feminism

To summarise, it seems that the fact that only women can become pregnant is a key factor in radical feminist theories of womanhood. It also feeds into arguments for Women-Only spaces. In the same way, men cannot become pregnant, and so are clearly separate from women. Arguments about whether bodily characteristics play important roles in distinguishing women from men in terms of identity are yet to be covered. In the literature, radical feminists argue that the capacity for childbirth significantly distinguishes women from men, and that only women can be involved in feminist politics as this is directed at male oppression.

Some radical feminists, however, argue that only women can be involved in feminist struggles and that it is impossible for a woman to be a feminist even if she orally agrees with feminist views. The view that feminist communities can be women-only is known as radical feminist separatism. Radical feminists, such as Greer, argue that patriarchy could only be effectively challenged in a society of women, by those who have been oppressed by their connection with men. Hence, it is said, women are justified in excluding men from feminist battles, in order to create such female-only spaces.

Men are not a woman, and hence are incapable of being the subject of patriarchal oppression. Moreover, men create, benefit from, and maintain oppressive power structures, to the detriment of women. Morally, women should therefore prioritize their own concerns over those of men, as they must reform the structures of society which affect women.

3.1. Waves of feminism

The first wave of feminism took place in the United States from about 1890 to 1920. In a sense, its time frame could be considered even broader than this. Before the contemporary U.S. feminist movement, American social activists interested in female equality and/or voting rights, women's historians and others began to use the term "first wave" long after the ratification of the 19th Amendment. Initially, the leaders of the first wave focused almost exclusively on the issue of voting rights and viewed it as a means of empowering women. Members of the first wave of feminism viewed females as rational, competent human beings, at least as capable as men of possessing the right to vote in national elections. Further, except for the outlying thoughts from certain commentators, the concept of female voting rights was not limited to the relatively liberal-minded first-wave feminists. Indeed in the U.S., the growing belief that every adult individual should have the right to vote was gathering momentum.

The feminist movement in the U.S. has gone through cycles of feminist activity. These waves include the first wave, the second wave, the third wave, and the fourth wave. The first wave took place in the U.S. in the early 20th century. The first-wave activists were very active and in addition to voting rights also dealt with issues of sexual equality, divorce, property rights, and birth control. The second wave was divided into the early second wave (1940s-1950s) and the later second wave (1960-1980). During the early second wave, actions involved professional work and wage differentials. The later second wave differed significantly from the early second wave. Although its major foundation remained equality with men, broader issues of female experiences began to define later second wave feminism as well. The third wave emerged from the mid-1990s and focused primarily on redefining what it meant to be a woman. The fourth wave can be dated to the mid-2010s and followed in the footsteps of the third wave by exploring female identity (and its often interactive and complex relationships) through the lens of feminism versus a particular racial or socio-economic background.

3.2. Intersectionality

In the 1977 book "The Black Woman," there, intersectional analysis looks to multiple grounds of identity that mutually constitute the self, engaging Kim's "personal standpoint" of her racial, gender, and, to a lesser but significant extent, economic position within the capitalist world-system across a range of social spaces (e.g. the family, the workforce, the broader African American community) and in relation to the institutional operations of several linked systems, such as the racial apparatuses by which society constructs and then resource-distributes and gender by which it governs difference in practice. Demographically (and, one might imagine, rhetorically), this orienting concept has since been foundational to the passing of feminist theory towards feminist studies of intersectionality and, ultimately, to a broader disciplinary acknowledgement of the phenomenological implications of the institutional mediation of individual identities, including as "scholars from various labelings and social concerns historically underrepresented in the academy and in social science research. It is now commonplace to consider identity as intersectional to some extent – as generated not by any one axis of subjection but by a combined operation of many. With Kim's point in mind, though, it is useful to note that these "many" are most often seen through the lens of those same few: gender, race, class, sexuality, and nation, as well as these few's regional or subcultural specifics (e.g. "urban" versus "rural," "Norwegian" versus "Kenyan"). This emphasis must be contextualised within the particular concerns of the United States academy (as well as the queer theory roots of many decontextualised concepts) and, especially, of US feminist literary criticism, which has sometimes been slow to engage with Kim's richer theoretical groundwork due to its overly narrow focus upon Foucault's investment in a depersonalised notion of power as intrinsically biopolitical, by the privileged ways in which many scholars themselves embody identities often flattened within the United States pan-racial binary, and/or by the anxiety that the complex lived realities enabled by the Black feminist tradition's theorisation of identity-as-intersectional can actually be addressed by the text.

3.3. *Feminist movements*

The importance of women joining together was expressed by the feminist movements during the 19th century on women's rights. They realized that it was essential to inspire other women and therefore participation to get the right, and should their gain be of any significance. A Norwegian gender historian says, when today's feminists talk about this, they often emphasize that it was about sharing experiences, providing identity, vision development, and action. It is the women's movement of the 70s that once again literally brought the word gender onto the agenda and invested it with the same significance that class had for the left in the 50s and 60s. Of course, it cannot be said that sexism doesn't exist just because men were not aware of it earlier, the knowing about historical constructions of gender and sex is only a prior condition in order to live in a gender-equal manner or... does not exist.

Modern feminist movements in the middle part of the 20th century have often defined women as "that share of society disadvantaged and exploited by the male sex." But it's a time when women's situation in the labor market and their political and human rights coincided largely with the problems that appeared on, for example, committee reports. Thus, the feminist demands for women's rights also spread to other spheres of life. The church man's differentiated language, stressing that "God evaluates the human being irrespective of sex, age, race, or social position. This means that it is to speak for the right of the voiceless, to condemn all forms of power and prejudice over other people - often made in the name of or defended with references to their faith," is likewise maintained in our time. Then follows a synthesis which links language, power, and discrimination together in a straight line showing it as a complex tool of oppression which in turn generates even more oppression, i.e. the feminist movements of today.

CHAPTER 4

Stereotypes and Misconceptions

In the case of women, the most common stereotypes usually involve physical strength, as certain activities may be considered too heavy for "weak" women. The education they receive is subservient and based on the idea that they have a weakness: crying. The traditional representations of women have been consolidated as slaves associated with emotional, empathetic and sensitive weaknesses. So girls are taught from an early age to be docile, tolerating, sensitive and polite. Once again, these are only labels that lead to a conditioning that later translates into problems related to self-abuse, anxiety, depression, isolation, lack of professional ambition, relationship instability, and others.

Stereotypes are misconceptions or false ideas, often in the form of a fixed image of a certain category of person, group or element. They are not always negative, but they are always narrow, selective and discriminatory because they reflect labels reinforced by social, ideological, cultural, racial, national, economic, political and even religious characteristics. The most common stereotypes regarding women are that they should be taken care of: their role is restricted to the reproductive, productive and nurturing processes, especially in the familial context. In the work environment, because it is difficult for society to understand women as entities just like men, with a voice and work skills, it is believed that they are beings who must be protected or who, paradoxically, may not be able to offer enough support.

4.1. Media portrayal

Traditionally, media portrayals of women center around stereotypically feminine traits. Women have been traditionally portrayed as more emotional, submissive, mild-tempered, delicate, and neurotic. They are also often described in terms of how well they embody domestic roles: they are mothers or caregivers. For example, Babcock et al. found that women who were shown the stereotype-disconfirming trait were not only perceived more negatively and less willing to lead, but also less willing to help out. Other work suggests that women might be underrepresented in the media overall, so there could be limitations to the ability to portray not only traditional roles but non-traditional roles too.

One major role of the media is to reflect and shape cultural norms. This is particularly true when it comes to the portrayal of women, who have been shown to be underrepresented across various media. For example, research shows that men tend to have more speaking roles in movies, especially in relation to professors, lawyers, medical doctors, and investigators in crime scenes. Additionally, films tend to pass the Bechdel test if there is a male producer, screenwriter, or director on the film, and it usually passes the test when the film is directed by a woman. In 2017, women were "missing" from 28% of all 100 top-grossing films in contrast to men who were "missing" from only 1%. The representation gap was even higher for women of color. Also, in 2020, the Center for the Study of Women in Television and Film pointed out that women were more likely to be shown in domestic scenarios than working, as well as in situations of personal tragedy or violence, and to be used as props by men.

4.2. Gender norms

The leading tenet of contemporary biology is that sex is indivisible while gender has two parts, and that the sex we discover befalls of women and men's apparently indissoluble differences of behaviour. Another founding tenet is that the largely trivial colours which signal reproductive availability to men are the leading causes of the division of the sexes: the consequence of the pressures of sexual selection has been, in particular species, to modify the more durable and more variable bodies of the female; this has led to profound histological and physiological adaptations which makes it impossible to sustain the life of the fittest baby without the daily attention of its mother; it is her particular form that assures at once the constitution of their offspring and the servo-mechanisms which put her in a position of xenic or reproductive inferiority.

Gender norms are otherwise arbitrary behavioural patterns which individuals are expected to accumulate or acquire because of their sex. Necessarily these are negative evaluations of the behaviours of those who do not conform to these patterns, typically women and men who behave as the sex they do not seem to be or the sex which would not be assigned to them as infants. So, gender norms are not captions applied from without to a neutral body; they are integral to the sexed body. It is not then that women are created by gender norms; rather the bodies of women are themselves gender norms.

4.3. Impact on society

According to this viewpoint, the superiority of the female, the mediation she offers between natural physicality and cultural spirituality, gives her an essential role within the social order: to call attention to this role is not so much to flatter the female as to defend the primacy of the social over economics. The later value of the cross-section of society that qualifies for eugenic respect rests on the theory of the female as "society's guardian," as Gurney once put it. More consistently and extensively, Albert Schäffle wrote up the argument supporting the conclusion that, because "woman and mother have become the life-source principle of our ethico-social order," it is families producing the "most accomplished mothers" who accounted for "the very essence of the State."

Are women "vital" to society? Sexual differences and the idea that women are "vital" to society provided grounds for rejection of utilitarian justifications of the inequality. Women were not happier than before emancipation, they argue, although while they were still necessary for sustaining life, they had to live among those who spurned them. "Women are vital for their own sake, and this source of looking at them should bring us happiness," declared Christine de Pisan. It is in women, explained Bodin, that men find intelligence, wisdom, and justice in their mothers, hospitality, providing, and care in their wives, chastity, and modesty in their daughters. "Polity cannot be maintained," insisted John Sprint, "but even formally be allowed, with the greatest necessity and concern engaged about women and their education."

CHAPTER 5

Women's Rights

Feminism: Each of the four feminist "waves" was born by the denial of the practical implementation of gender equality in daily life. The first wave of the feminist movement began with the Seneca Falls Women's Rights Convention in 1848, promoted especially by Elizabeth Cady Stanton and Susan B. Anthony, bringing to an end the first wave with the granting of women's suffrage in the United States of America in 1920. From the gathering in ways to act and think that supposedly differ by sex, some began to question the reverse of such differences. These approached women's rights as human rights as argued in the 1792 Declaration of the Rights of Woman and of the Female Citizen. They argued that sex acted as a barrier to equal opportunities (called sexual discrimination) in the fields of policy, public life, professional life, education, marriage and economic rights. A woman needed the right to education and of holding public office. Women had to be given the right to a fair trial. Any distinction between men and women had to be based on solely in virtue.

It is necessary to review the women's rights movement and its development in the past 150 years in addressing the fundamental questions posed by the subject of this article; beginning with discussions in the mid-nineteenth century of the treatment of women, it moved to the subject of distinguishing between the sexes and then to more complex issues, until culminating in the fifth wave of feminist struggle. Today, there are and there will be many people who fear that the struggles to date will end up being futile at the hands of a minority; however, will the issue not continue to regain importance while women continue to be treated less favorably than men? There was a time when owners had more rights than slaves, but the natural course of evolution led to a stage characterized by the full guarantee of the rights of each of these.

5.1. Legal rights

The assignation of sex to a body, and the difference between what is normal and what is abnormal in pointing to males or females consists of all the scientific evidence that is examined and weighed in the light of scientific and clinico-anatomical evidence. Sex is based on the conjoint appearance of the external genitalia, the chromosomal pattern and the gonadal histology. Examinations like no anatomic human origin or hermaphrodite morphology, testicles, scrotal raphe, phallus, male aspect and clitoris have clitoral hypertrophy or are absent for female appearance. This leads to the ineluctable conclusion that, in most cases, the presence of normal male anatomy determines males, and normal female anatomy supplies evidence and doesn't determine femaleness. However, the use of sex has a descriptive feature due to hermaphroditism in a theoretical approach.

Through appeals to biology, the Virginia Supreme Court has maintained that assignment of sex and understanding of gender based on anatomy are legal rights, which may under some circumstances be stronger than constitutional protections of personal expression. The court has ruled that women may be required to wear skirts and dresses, even when men are permitted to wear the same attire. A female wearing a tuxedo was a woman, in the eyes of the U.S. Supreme Court, but not in the eyes of the Little Sisters court, which concluded that the case was an easy one: where the lower court had found that a tuxedo much more effectively obscured appellant's anatomy than when a skirt and blouse were worn, appellant was not being required to dress as a female, let alone to bear any professional stigma or to make herself uniquely vulnerable to sexual assault, hindering access in her chosen occupation. The word female thus means that which is typically considered female (or perhaps may be made to appear so) within the context in question.

5.2. Reproductive rights

Many disputes across the globe revolve around whether women's right to autonomy and reproductive self-determination should be recognized. For example, UN committee member Jodi L. Jacobson voices her dissatisfaction at "the perception of us as 'victims' of reproductive rights abuses, a perception that underlies and shapes the debates at the United Nations, and around which the Cairo debate has largely been conducted" and stressed that "[t]here can be no contraceptive technology, no abortion, no desire for carrying forward freedom without some level of justice in the world." Proponents of the position that a woman is a fully formed adult human individual are often sidelined by other feminists loyal to a version of feminism that considers the surge of this ideal to be dangerous and the expansion of female reproductive rights to be capable of burdening and impeding the march of progress.

Reproductive rights have been an important battleground in the sex/gender wars. The 1994 International Conference on Population and Development in Cairo recommended "that all countries review and revise their laws in order to integrate equality in the family, with equal rights of women and men." The 1995 Fourth World Conference on Women in Beijing recommended that "reproductive health ... implies that people are able to have a satisfying and safe sex life and that they have the capability to reproduce and the freedom to decide if, when, and how often to do so." A few decades later, the Declaration on the Occasion of the 25th Anniversary of the Fourth World Conference on Women calls for "reproductive justice for women, adolescents, and girls, and all individuals with the ability to bear children." The statement was issued by France's Ministry of Europe and Foreign Affairs.

5.3. Workplace equality

Justice Ginsburg learned a great deal from teaching Dale a "taxed anachronism". But he was also a poet. Her 1966 Oberlin course, which marked the first time Ohio students were introduced to the then-recent Ginsburg brief, is titled "The Law, the subjugation of Women." she proposes to teach the students to appreciate the dynamic possibilities of the Fourteenth Amendment's Equal Protection Clause, which "spreads its concepts over a manifold universe of sordidly and groups." A world that transcends class distinction (and class distinctions). It all but transcends rope and gender distinctions because of the universals that are all related to human interests and worth. A progressive tax creates rubbing at the margin through the loss of tax revenue caused by a decreased work speed. But we accept a greatest-explorer solution if it confronts polating a Roth progression not family taxes and we are only splitting atoms in bills we have also in the wider world. Meanwhile, Oberlin and Roybits first enroll in a US stimulated class at Georgetown Law, and Roybits cooperates as a research assistant on a company tax and US class of fridge.

Workplace equality Justice Ginsburg demonstrated that the prohibition against sex discrimination worked against old stereotypes through cases that not only involved her husband whom she married in 1954, but other men who had suffered from the stereotype. This is also true of her equality work as a whole. An example will help to illustrate this point. In my earliest college memory, I am walking around the campus, avoiding eye contact with anyone, when a woman appears on the other side of the street. She is an apple orchard effulgence of red and stars. I want to look at her, but students say things about beauty not having hearts; looking at her will send her into orbit.